The second Fort Union (Star Fort) was an earthwork fortification, built to defend against Confederate troops.

volunteers from New Mexico, labored around the clock in four-hour shifts to build the earthen enclosure. The four corners of the "star" enabled the artillery within to provide overlapping supporting fire to one another.

Despite these preparations, the Star Fort never received a Rebel assault. In March 1862 the fort was bolstered by Colonel John Slough's First Colorado Regiment. Slough's force of Colorado and New Mexico volunteers and U.S. regular troops took the fight to the Confederates, defeating them in a two-day engagement near Santa Fe.

The Star Fort was even less comfortable than the decaying first fort. The bunker-like quarters were damp and considered unhealthy. Most of the troops lived in tent camps outside the earth walls. Fort Union's status as a "permanent" garrison and depot called for a more substantial facility. General James Carleton won approval for improvements, and the Star Fort was abandoned.

The Third Fort. In 1863 construction began on the final, and largest Fort Union. It consisted of three autonomous facilities: the post of Fort Union, the massive Fort Union

Quartermaster Depot, and the Fort Union Arsenal. Completed after five years of construction and at a cost of over one million dollars, the third fort remained active until 1891.

Hundreds of civilians worked to build the fort. Adobe bricks were laid on stone foundations, allowed to settle, and the completed structures were then plastered. Porches, fences, and street lamps were added. A determined, but

futile, attempt to grow trees and grass on the parade ground was made. The author of an 1867 inspection report declared the officers' quarters to be "far better than any . . . I have seen at any other frontier post." But by 1876, the quarters were plagued with leaks and bulging walls.

The new post was designed to garrison four companies of infantry or cavalry. Each company was housed in a U-shaped barrack that included a dormitory, kitchen, dining room, storage rooms, orderly room, and a reading room, a rarity for its time.

Two additional sets of barracks were erected in 1876. Fort Union was then a six-company post, which made it one of the larger garrisons west of the Mississippi.

The hospital complex was one of the first areas constructed at the new post. Completed in 1864, its three wards contained a total of thirty-six beds. Surrounding structures included latrines, a wood house, cisterns, laundry, bathhouse, "dead" house (mortuary), and quarters for the hospital matron and hospital steward. The latter was an enlisted man who served both as a physician's assistant and administrator.

Post Trader's Complex. West of the post officers' quarters stood a number of structures used by the post sutler, or, (as the name was designated in 1866) post "trader." Post traders, appointed by the secretary of war, monopolized a general store on the military post and provided goods and services not normally available through army supply channels. Household goods, toiletries, textiles, food, and beverages formed the bulk of the stock. The trader system was the forerunner to the "post exchange" on military posts.

Additions to the Fort Union post trader complex in the 1860s and 1870s included a hotel, restaurant, bowling

alley, and saloon. Anyone on the post or passing through could frequent the store and its environs.

Prices were set by a board of army officers of the post, yet, despite this supposed safeguard, prices at most army garrisons remained notoriously high throughout the frontier period, in part due to high transportation costs. The sale of alcohol at inflated prices helped keep post trader operations profitable.

The post trader system was open to political manipulation and abuse, and

Samuel D. Raymond of the First Colorado Battery fought in the battle at Glorietta Pass

Post quartermaster's depot under construction.

led to the 1876 impeachment of Secretary of War William Belknap for selling traderships. Fort Union's post trader at that time was John Dent, a brother-in-law of President Ulysses S. Grant.

Quartermaster's Depot. As the general depot for military supplies entering the Southwest, the quartermaster's operation at Fort Union was, during the years of the early fort, housed in log huts, tents, and even under tarpaulins. But the third fort included a massive depot of permanent buildings designed to properly house this huge operation. Construction began in 1863, and was completed in 1867.

Built around a parade ground (which was merely cosmetic, since the depot had no assigned force) was a row of quarters for the depot quartermaster and his subordinate officers, along with offices for the depot and the officer in charge of procuring and issuing food. Facing these was a line of warehouses and maintenance shops for storage, repairs, and fabrication.

By the time the new depot became operational, the Mountain Branch had gained in popularity over the Cimarron Cutoff to become the primary route of the Santa Fe Trail. Between two and three thousand wagons plying the trail each year were contract trains hauling military goods, and most of these ended their trip at the Fort Union Depot. Wagons were unloaded at storehouse docks, where the quartermaster and his staff inventoried, unpacked, inspected, and stored the goods. These goods were then repacked and sent to other posts as needed.

The depot work force, which numbered as many as seven hundred in 1867, was made up primarily of local civilians, plus depot officers and a very few noncommissioned officers. Stark, one-room apartments were provided for quartermaster employees. A long row of them faced the storehouses on the west and the transportation corral on the east.

To deliver materials from the Fort Union Depot the army did much of its own hauling. Unlike the oxen used by most civilian freighters, mules were the army's "prime movers," due to their greater speed. Hundreds of them were cared for in a massive corral. The depot also had a large force of wagonmasters, teamsters, and wagons, which necessitated shops and mechanics capable of repairing or totally rebuilding army wagons. The mechanic's corral was the center of this activity.

The depot machine shop was built

A ration cart assembled from condemned parts and hitched to a white donkey amused fort residents.

The mechanic's corral.

(Above) The completed post officers' quarters were superior to most in the West but nevertheless were beset with leaky roofs and falling plaster. (Right) Lydia Spencer Lane (seated) in 1867.

The Fort Union Baseball Club

Fort Union arsenal around 1879.

The trader's store.

TRADERS STORE

Grand Old Man of the Arsenal. When Colonel Sumner arrived to build Fort Union in 1851, he brought with him Military Storekeeper William Raule Shoemaker, in charge of ordnance or the Ninth Military Department. Shoemaker never left Fort Union. A supreme diplomat, he maintained his distance from the petty quarrels that would engulf the post commander and depot quartermaster over the next quarter of a century. As commander of the Fort Union Arsenal he saw to his own affairs and saw to it that his men did likewise.

At the outbreak of the Civil War, many Fort Union officers of Southern birth openly spoke of turning Fort Union over to the Rebel cause. Shoemaker declared his loyalty to the Union, promptly entrenched his arsenal, and prepared to destroy it, but the revolt never materialized.

Devastated by the death of his wife Julia in 1863, Shoemaker chose to remain close to her grave. He commanded the arsenal from 1851 until it was closed in 1882, having witnessed fully half of the old Santa Fe Trail days. Staying on as unofficial caretaker at his beloved arsenal buildings, he died on September 17, 1886, and was buried next to Julia.

in 1866 and contained machinery for sawing, planing, and mortising wood. A fence enclosed lumber supplies. Because of the danger of fire, this facility was isolated several hundred yards north of the depot commissary storehouse.

The Fort Union Depot remained an important and active operation into the early 1880s. But beginning in 1865, the Atchison, Topeka, and Santa Fe Railroad moved west, and finally passed Fort Union at nearby Watrous in 1879. With the railroad then so deep into the territory and overland trips on the Santa Fe Trail that much shortened, maintaining a depot at Fort Union no longer made sense. Slowly, the supplies and functions were transferred elsewhere. In 1883 the buildings were put to other uses and the depot ceased to operate.

The Arsenal. In addition to a quartermaster depot, the first fort also had an ordnance depot. With the construction of the third fort, the original site became an "ordnance reserve," and new buildings were erected.

Officially termed an "arsenal" in the mid-1860s, the facility received arms, accoutrements, ammunition, and related equipment. The arsenal processed and stored these items, and distributed them to other Southwestern posts. It also received and stored excess and obsolete weaponry, made repairs, and served as a clearinghouse for the ordnance business in the Department of New Mexico. Both soldiers and civilians worked at the Fort Union Arsenal. The soldiers were some of a very few men of the Ordnance Department stationed on the frontier.

Life at the Fort. The 1880s ushered in an era quite different from Fort Union's first three decades. By now, much of New Mexico's frontier was tamed and the railroad had replaced the Santa Fe Trail. However, the garrison grew larger than it ever had been, primarily because the post offered badly needed housing for inactive troops.

Garrison life was monotonous and boring. The daily routine was an endless

Genevieve LaTourette recalled her Fort Union home as "most comfortable."

succession of roll calls, fatigue duties, retreat parades, and guard-mounting ceremonies. For many, homemade entertainment and social gaiety filled off-duty hours, in an attempt to quell the boredom of inactivity.

Other Fort Union residents noted the difficulties of frontier life. Lydia Spencer Lane, a frequent traveler on the Santa Fe Trail, was the first occupant of the new third fort commanding officers' quarters, along with her children and husband, Colonel William B. Lane. She remembered her new quarters as imposing in appearance, "but there was no comfort in them." She despised the fine dust that settled everywhere, the lack of basic furnishings,and the inability to hire or keep reliable domestic help. One evening shortly after occupying her new quarters, the plaster on

The Twenty-Third Infantry Band posed in 1883 against buildings that were already deteriorating.

A Fort Union Couple. On the third of August, 1873, Private Patrick Cloonan of Company B of the Eighth U.S. Cavalry married Bridget Molloy at Fort Union. Both had come from Ireland to seek a better life and had found each other in the process.

Cloonan completed his first enlistment in April, Colonel J. Irvin Gregg signing the character section of Cloonan's discharge with the notation, "An excellent soldier and most reliable man." On December 11, Col. Gregg promoted Cloonan to corporal and, just two months later, to sergeant. It must have been during this brief period that Corporal Cloonan posed for this portrait in full-dress uniform.

Bridget supplemented the family income by working as one of the laundresses for Company B, and her photo is one of the very few known to exist of one to serve in the army's only position authorized for women.

The Cloonans, along with Company B, departed Fort Union in January, 1876. After ten years of army service, Sergeant Cloonan took his final discharge in April, 1878.

her dining room ceiling collapsed as she served supper.

Yet Fort Union enjoyed luxuries unknown to smaller posts. Its size often permitted its designation as a regiment's headquarters, the trappings of which included the regimental band. Rapid mail service from the East was possible because the Barlow and Sanderson stage line ran past the fort. The growing city of Las Vegas, twenty-eight miles away, offered occasional entertainment and a nearby hot spring bathing facility.

Few enlisted men in the Regular Army were married, and the army discouraged marriage in several ways. A soldier first needed the permission of his commanding officer and then had to deal with the fact that few frontier posts had quarters for married soldiers. Hovels and shanties of every description sprang up on military posts, forming districts often termed "sudsville" or "suds row," in reference to the laundry work performed by the wives of so many soldiers. But soldiers assigned to Fort Union found that housing *was* available for enlisted families, a rare luxury then.

Career-minded enlisted men could aspire to eventual appointment to the noncommissioned staff as technician and specialist representatives of staff corps—post ordnance sergeant, hospital steward, commissary sergeant, or, after 1884, post quartermaster sergeant (roughly equivalent to today's warrant officer). Members of the band also could count on a life of increased status and lifestyle.

Company B, Tenth Infantry

Faces of the Troops. A collection of glass plate negatives in the Kansas State Historical Society reveals an astounding group of Fort Union views from 1887. The entire assigned garrison of the fort had posed for group portraits. At the time, the Fort Union garrison consisted of Companies B, C, D, F, and I of the Tenth Infantry, and Troop E, Sixth Cavalry. Close examination reveals much about these units and the men in them.

The Regular Army of that period was not a young one. The "peach-fuzz" faces so prevalent in portraits of Civil War volunteer units are mixed with those of men who have seen much of life. The images also suggest discipline varied from company to company. Some companies included pets and children with the group, along with cooks who appear as though they just stepped out of the kitchen, images that remind one of a family portrait rather than a stiff military scene. Other companies fall more into the latter category. The two with the greatest degree of military bearing include a commissioned officer (evidenced by shoulder straps), which may well account for the formal poses.

Troop E had at least four exposures made, using both mounted and dismounted poses. In the latter are more men without horses than with. Troop E

Troop E, Sixth Cavalry

may well have had a shortage of mounts, not an uncommon situation among cavalry units.

Decline of the Fort. In the 1887 photos of Fort Union, one can see the decline of this major western outpost already well underway. Tight military budgets of the time meant that appropriations to keep the structures in proper repair were never made, and the buildings literally began to crumble from the day they were completed. By 1887 the buildings were totally devoid of their original plaster covering, and the walls were eroded and cracked, requiring bracing in many places. While the fort would not be abandoned for another four years, many structures were unused because of poor condition.

In 1890 the Census Bureau declared that there was no longer a definable line of settlement in the West; as Frederick Jackson Turner pointed out in 1893, this event signalled the end of the "frontier." For many years the army's goal had been to consolidate what were frontier-based units into large posts convenient to rail transportation and Indian reservations, the most likely scenes of trouble. This was not feasible until the mid-1880s, and then it took several years to put into effect, largely due to lack of money. But Fort Union did not meet the criteria to be one of the consolidation centers.

On February 21, 1891, Company C and Company H, Tenth Infantry, marched to nearby Watrous and boarded a special train to Fort Wingate, their new station. Ten men from each company remained to pack and ship government property. Finally, on May 15, they departed, leaving behind them the once-great military terminus of the Santa Fe Trail. Fort Union, along with the frontier that had created it, passed into history.

Fort Union Today. Today the ruins of Fort Union are preserved by the National Park Service as a national monument, part of the Santa Fe National Historic Trail. An adobe masonry crew preserves and stabilizes the ruins, constantly battling the forces of wind, rain, and snow that toppled the buildings originally.

A Soldier and Comrades. In 1884 Niels J. C. Larsen, a young Danish immigrant, enlisted in the U.S. Army and shortly thereafter found himself in Troop G, Sixth Cavalry, chasing will-o'-the-wisp Apaches in southern New Mexico. After Geronimo's surrender in September 1886, Troop G was transferred to the more serene surroundings of Fort Union. Because the post was full to capacity of five companies of the Tenth Infantry, Troop G set up housekeeping at the former Fort Union Arsenal site. They took advantage of photographer J. R. Riddle's 1888 visit.

Larsen must have been a sentimentalist. His photo collection includes dozens of images of chums he served with at different posts throughout his career. Unfortunately, he failed to pencil individual identities on the photos.

Troop G made a hurried departure from Fort Union in December 1890, as the entire Sixth Cavalry was sent to the Pine Ridge, South Dakota country to help quell the Sioux "ghost dance" fever. These men witnessed the last scene in the last act of the tragedy that was America's Indian Wars.